Pet Care

Fish

Dash!
LEVELED READERS
An Imprint of Abdo Zoom • abdobooks.com

1

Dash!
LEVELED READERS

Level 1 – Beginning
Short and simple sentences with familiar words or patterns for children who are beginning to understand how letters and sounds go together.

Level 2 – Emerging
Longer words and sentences with more complex language patterns for readers who are practicing common words and letter sounds.

Level 3 – Transitional
More developed language and vocabulary for readers who are becoming more independent.

abdobooks.com

Published by Abdo Zoom, a division of ABDO, PO Box 398166, Minneapolis, Minnesota 55439.
Copyright © 2019 by Abdo Consulting Group, Inc. International copyrights reserved in all countries.
No part of this book may be reproduced in any form without written permission from the publisher.
Dash!™ is a trademark and logo of Abdo Zoom.

Printed in the United States of America, North Mankato, Minnesota.
092018
012019

Photo Credits: iStock, Shutterstock
Production Contributors: Kenny Abdo, Jennie Forsberg, Grace Hansen, John Hansen
Design Contributors: Dorothy Toth, Neil Klinepier

Library of Congress Control Number: 2018946192

Publisher's Cataloging in Publication Data

Names: Murray, Julie, author.
Title: Fish / by Julie Murray.
Description: Minneapolis, Minnesota : Abdo Zoom, 2019 | Series: Pet care |
    Includes online resources and index.
Identifiers: ISBN 9781532125225 (lib. bdg.) | ISBN 9781641856676 (pbk.) |
    ISBN 9781532126246 (ebook) | ISBN 9781532126758 (Read-to-me ebook)
Subjects: LCSH: Aquarium fishes--Juvenile literature. | Fishes as pets--Juvenile
    literature. | Pets--Juvenile literature.
Classification: DDC 639.34--dc23

Table of Contents

Fish

Fish make great pets. They come in many colors and sizes. Jade picks out a new fish.

5

Fish need a tank. It needs to have a **water filter** and a light.

Pebbles should cover the bottom of the tank. Plants make good hiding spots.

The water is important! Be sure to check the **pH levels**. Put special drops in the water to keep your fish healthy.

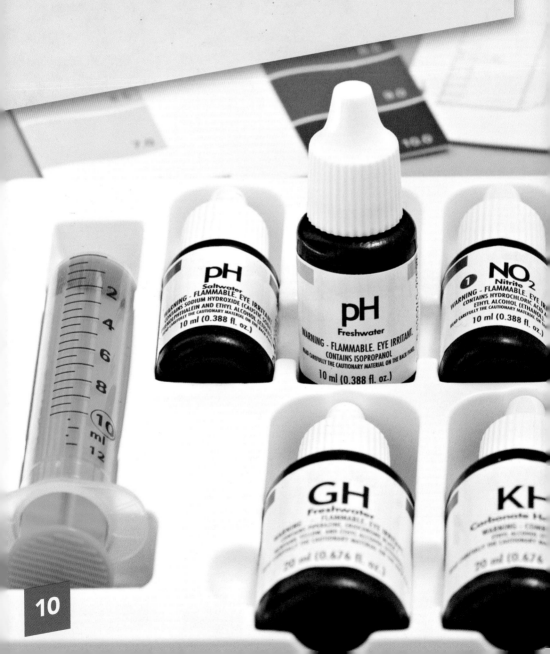

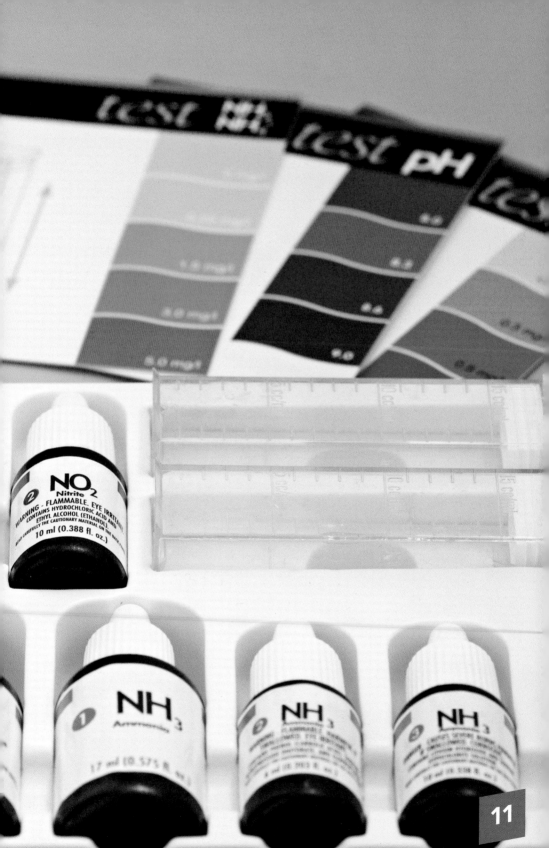

Fish need to be fed daily. They mainly eat fish flakes. A few sprinkles each day is enough.

The tank needs to be kept clean. This should be done weekly. The **pebbles** should be cleaned each month.

Many fish live in fresh water.
Goldfish live in fresh water.

Some fish live in salt water.
Clownfish are saltwater fish.

Fish are fun pets. Andy watches his fish swim all day long!

Things Fish Need

- A clean tank

- Plants for hiding

- Water

- Fish food

Glossary

pebbles – small rocks.

pH level – a measure from 1-14 of the acidity or alkalinity of water soluble substances. Saltwater fish prefer an alkaline pH of 8.0 or above. Freshwater fish prefer it to be between 5.5 and 7.5.

water filter – removes impurities by lowering the contamination of water.

Index

Online Resources

Booklinks
NONFICTION NETWORK
FREE! ONLINE NONFICTION RESOURCES

To learn more about fish care, please visit **abdobooklinks.com**. These links are routinely monitored and updated to provide the most current information available.